1+ ,- J

CALM THE

CHAOTIC MIND

**Correct Thinking Mistakes, Worry
Less & Find Calm Amid The Chaos**

KUNAL DUDEJA

© *Calm The Chaotic Mind*
Kunal Dudeja
1st Edition
All rights reserved
Publication Date: June 2022
ISBN: 9798815637788
Published by:
Adhyyan Books
Office No. 125,
Opposite Vivanta by Taj,
DDA SFS. Pocket-1, Dwarka,
Sec-22, New Delhi-110077
Website: http://adhyyanbooks.com
E-mail: contact@adhyyanbooks.com

Introduction

Calm The Chaotic Mind presents you with a gamut of practical, tried, tested and unique methods to calm your mind during chaotic situations. EFT, CBT, Breathwork, Thinking Corrections, Self-Acceptance, Shifting Core Beliefs, Power of Gratitude and Forgiveness are some of the profound techniques presented in this book to calm your emotions and correct your thinking and thereby improve your emotional well-being. Some of the methods are proactive and designed to create a calm and peaceful lifestyle.

If you do not know anything about these techniques, you would still be able to learn and apply them to bring in positive changes in your day-to-day living. I have removed the complexity from some chapters by including audio files to help you implement the techniques easily. If the files do not open for some reason, please do not be disappointed. You will still be able to implement the methods with some practice.

By the way, are you curious about the 1+1 becoming 3? I think you are. So let me give you the answer. 1+1 became 3 because I made a thinking error. That's Right! Not a typing error, not a calculation error but a thinking error. We all make such thinking errors on a regular basis. Some of thoughts within these thinking errors –

"I am not feeling good today; hence it's a bad day", "I lost my keys; hence I am irresponsible!", "Since I am kind to you, you should also be kind to me.", "My mother is not happy. It must be because of me.," My nose is so big that no one will love me.", "Either I am on a strict diet, or I will eat everything", "I forgot to wish my father on his birthday, I am a terrible daughter".

If you relate to this thinking, then you possibly are making such errors. Such thinking mistakes can create chaos in the mind if not corrected over time. The good news is you can learn to identify and correct them. While part 1 of this book aims to empower you with easy to implement techniques to be calm, the part 2 of this book aims to train you to understand and correct such thinking mistakes. In part 2 you also learn one of my All Time Go To technique – Emotional Freedom Technique also known as Tapping. Part 3 is to upgrade the Peace quotient of your life with proactive ways to be calm and peaceful.

Dedication

This book is dedicated to you.

With the teachings in this book, I aim to empower you to get better at managing your emotions and correcting your thoughts. I intend that you create the ability to be calm and at ease (as much as possible and as quickly as possible) amid various life situations.

I hope I can make a positive contribution to your life with book.

Disclaimer

This book does not provide any medical advice nor prescribe any technique to treat physical, emotional, mental, and medical problems. For any medical, physical, emotional, or mental issues, please consult your physician, counsellor, or mental health practitioner as you consider appropriate. This book intends to offer information of a generic nature for your spiritual evolution. If you use any of the book's information for yourself, the author assumes no responsibility for your actions. The reader of this book must take complete responsibility for its use. Further, the author offers the information in this book solely as his opinion and not necessarily the view of any of the founders of EFT and CBT. Readers are strongly cautioned and advised to consult with a physician, psychologist, psychiatrist, or other licensed health care professional before using any of the information in this book. The author, publisher and contributors of this book and other parties related to this book (a) explicitly disclaim any liability for and shall not be liable for any loss or damage, including but not limited to the use of this information; (b) shall not be liable for any direct or indirect compensatory, special, incidental, or consequential damages or costs of any kind or character; (c) shall not be responsible for any acts or omission by any party including but not limited to any party mentioned or included in the information or otherwise (d) does not endorse or support any material or information from any party mentioned or included in the information or otherwise(e) will not be liable for damages or costs resulting from any claim whatsoever. If the reader or user does not agree with any of the foregoing terms, the reader or user should not use the information in this book to read it. A reader who continues reading this book will be deemed to have accepted the provisions of this disclaimer.

TABLE OF CONTENTS

TABLE OF CONTENTS (AUDIO LINKS)

PART 1

CALMING METHODS FOR EVERYDAY STRESSES

Chapter 1

Relax Quickly With
Conscious Breathing

"Breath is the bridge which connects life to consciousness, which unites your body to your thoughts. Whenever your mind becomes scattered, use your breath as the means to take hold of your mind again."— *Thich Nhat Hanh*

A simple to understand and easy to follow breathing technique that can help improve your physical, spiritual, and mental well-being. This technique can play a vital role in helping you become calmer from everyday stresses. Below are the steps to do it:

Step 1) Breathe in for 4 to 5 seconds
Step 2) Hold your breath for 4 to 5 seconds
Step 3) Breathe out for 4-5 seconds
Step 4) Hold your breath for 4-5 seconds

Based on your comfort, you can decide the number of seconds you wish to breathe in, hold and breathe out. I have noticed that the 4-5 seconds of breathing delivers good results.

You can use this technique when you want to focus or when highly stressed. Start by practising this technique for 2 minutes every 2 hours of your day and sail through your daily stresses.

I recommend, give it a go now, before you read the next chapter. Try to do it for 1 min and see how you feel.

Chapter 2

The 1 Minute Grounding Technique To Reduce Anxious Feelings

"Get yourself grounded, and you can navigate even the stormiest roads in peace." — *Steve Goodier.*

When our mind is all over the place, it is essential to do grounding to calm our minds. This technique brings you back to the present moment. The first step is to take a few calming breaths and start feeling relaxed and then apply this technique below: -

Step 1) Look at five things
Look around for five things and describe them in your mind. For example, you could tell them in your mind as - I see the pen, the book, the clock, etc.

Step 2) Touch & Feel four things
Touch and feel four things around you. For example, touch and feel the smooth cold surface of your desk, the soft touch of your pillow, the rough texture of your car seat, the texture of your watch etc.

Step 3) Acknowledge hearing three things
Without judging, hear sounds of three things - the distant traffic, the sound from your ceiling fan, your tummy rolling etc.

Step 4) Notice 2 things You Can smell
Try to smell the subtle fragrance of the air surrounding you
or your skin. Move to a different space and sniff something.

Step 5) Become Aware of 1 thing you can taste
The lingering taste of the coffee or mint after food. Try and
get to taste something you enjoy.

This grounding technique can help release anxious energy
from your body, grounding and calming you so you can
focus again and be fully present in the Here and Now. Take
your time and do all the 5 steps. Do not be in a rush initially.
With practice, do all the 5 steps in a minute and experience
the massive shifts in your wellbeing.

Chapter 3

Put (Uncertain) Things
into Perspective

"As far as the laws of mathematics refer to reality, they are not certain; and as far as they are certain, they do not refer to reality." — *Albert Einstein*

Uncertain future events could often get undue importance. If you are worried about a future uncertain event like Math exams, critical meeting, stage performance, you could tend to assume that things may not work out the way you anticipate.

Here is a simple yet profound technique to put things into perspective and for you to look at the facts and worry less about the future uncertain events.

Ask the below three questions about this uncertain event:

- Am I over-estimating the probability of this event occurring? (The probability of things going wrong)
- Am I over-estimating the impact occurring from this event? (The damage if things go wrong)
- Am I underestimating my ability to cope if it occurs? (My ability to handle if things would take a turn)

16

Most likely, you would answer as a YES for the above questions. Now ask the below questions to put this future uncertain event into perspective:

Q1) What is the likelihood of this event (things going to wrong) happening? Rate your likelihood
5 - Almost certain to happen
4- Very likely to happen
3- Equal probability that it may or may not happen
2- highly unlikely to happen
1 - Almost sure that it won't happen.

Q2) How bad would the impact be if the event occurred? Here you try to put the impact into a different perspective. For examples:
- It would be bad but not tragic.
- It would be difficult but not impossible.
- It would be frustrating but not intolerable.

Q3) How well would I use my coping ability if the event happened?
Here you would want to give yourself credit for handling and coping with the situation if the event occurs.
- I would feel sad but not entirely heartbroken.
- I may find it difficult but will be able to cope with it.
- I would be uncomfortable, but I will be able to stand it.

Q4) Are there any facts which can positively inspire me? Here, you may want to recall any facts that can positively inspire you and reduce your anxious feelings about this future event.

Let us take the example where you are about to give a speech to a large audience. You are worried that you may freeze during your address. Now answer the below questions:

Q1) What is the likelihood of me getting frozen during my speech?

5 - Almost certain to happen

4- Very likely to happen

3- Equal probability that it may or may not happen

2- *Highly unlikely to happen*

1 - Almost sure that it won't happen.

Q2) How bad would the impact be if I get frozen?

- It would be bad but not tragic.

Q3) How well would I use my coping ability if the event happened?

- I would be uncomfortable. However, I will be able to pull myself together.

Q4) Are there any facts which can positively inspire me?

- I am very confident about what I am going to speak
- I have the support of experts in case I fumble
- I have given a similar speech at least 20 times before (although to a small audience) and have received positive feedback.

When you start putting things and facts into perspective about the future event you are worried about, you can experience a positive change and become calmer.

Chapter 4

Eating Consciously

"We do food every single day! Conscious Eating is a big step toward Conscious Living. Quality and Quantity of Food is directly related to our Health and state of mind. We can use food to help us recover from Stress and Disease. Not taking food seriously will eventually lead to Stress or/and Disease."— Natasa Pantovic Nuit,

In continuation of the grounding technique, I share another excellent method that you can use to calm yourself and make your meal a pleasurable activity. So here is how it works. When you eat your food, look very closely at the colour of the food, notice the texture, and consciously notice what is going on inside your mouth. Feel the morsels of the food you are eating. If you take 15 minutes to have your meal, try to complete your dinner in 25-30 minutes. Eat slowly and enjoy your food. If you are on a weight loss diet and cannot control the cake craving, use this technique when you eat the cake. Eat slowly and enjoy it thoroughly. Be in the present moment. Be fully engaged in experiencing the taste of the cake. When you do this, you will be surprised that the quantum of cake you ate will be less than what you anticipated. You would receive the same amount of joy by eating a tiny piece of cake. Conscious eating allows your body to receive and enjoy the meal entirely. It also helps your body to slow down and be calmer.

Chapter 5

Calmness at Your Fingertips
(Quite Literally)

What if you could be calm in seconds just by touching your fingertips. Sounds exciting? Here is how it works - Anchoring is a valuable NLP (Neuro-Linguistic Programming) technique that helps you quickly get into the desired state using a past emotional reference. So, whether you want to be happy, confident, calm, peaceful, or enthusiastic, you can get into this state quickly in just a few seconds with practice. First, let us understand what an anchor is. An Anchor is a bookmark in our mind that triggers a specific memory and thus the emotion associated with that memory. You already have anchors. Those could be creating healthy or unhealthy emotions. You may not have created them consciously, but they got made subconsciously. For example, you could be walking down the road, and you see a red color car. It could remind you of a pleasant (or unpleasant) childhood memory. The memory could be where you had gone out with your family, and it was the best day of your life. Once you recollect that memory, you automatically feel happy. Similarly, when you happen to hold a flower, it may remind you of an old memory you had with your ex-boyfriend or ex-girlfriend, and it may create some sense of discomfort (or comfort based on what happened). So, to summarize, an anchor is nothing but a trigger in the form of a visual, touch, situation, gesture, smell, or thing which could trigger a memory resulting in pleasant or unpleasant emotions.

To experience the state of calmness in seconds, we will create an anchor which can make us calm in seconds. Once we make the anchor, we do not have to create it again. Once created, it gets stored in our subconscious.

Step 1 Identify a Gesture

The first step is to identify a gesture that will act as the trigger to be calm—like touching the thumb with your index finger or touching your ear lobe, or something similar. Once the gesture is identified and the calmness anchor created each time you execute the gesture, i.e., feel the ear lobe or touch the index finger with your thumb, you would experience calmness.

Step 2 Create the Anchor

Sit in a comfortable position with your eyes closed. (Since your eyes are closed, you can ask your friend to read the instructions as below)

1. Take five deep breaths and relax.
2. Recall a memory from your past where you were entirely calm and peaceful. Try and live that experience again.
3. See what you see.
4. Hear the words (if you or someone else is talking)
5. Hear the sounds (could be the air or the sea)
6. Feel the calmness in your heart and body.

7. Now that you are entirely living that moment, touch your ring finger with your thumb and squeeze it or execute your own anchor.

8. Do another squeeze and make the picture brighter this time. Again, the visuals appear closer and double the intensity of calmness.

You have created the anchor to be calm. You psychologically associate the neural signal of "two squeezes of your ring finger and thumb" with "Calmness".

GUIDELINES:

Do not create ten anchors all at once. Instead, create one anchor for the emotional state you wish to experience. Practice it for a couple of weeks and then make the new anchor.

If you do not remember being in a calm state, you can create a new imagination of what calmness means to you and follow the same steps.

Step 3 Execute the Anchor

Now that you have created the anchor for calm, you need to execute the anchor. Double squeeze the finger or touch the ear lobe or any other gesture you have made. Initially, you may require some mental effort; however, it will become an automatic process with practice.

Want a friend to help you create this Anchor?

Audio File: Create the Anchor to Be Calm

(Play it on speaker for effective results)

Chapter 6

One Joy Everyday

"Do good, live in the most positive and joyful way possible every day." — Roy T. Bennett

The pace of our life can be so fast that you could forget to get in touch with the little things which give immense joy and happiness. Therefore, it is essential to plan and execute the small pleasures every day. The golden rule is to do it every day. One joyful activity every day. Doing one joyful activity every day will make you calmer and at peace. Here is a suggestive list of activities:

To Combat Stress
Your favorite Hobby
Taking the dog out for a walk after work
Taking a luxurious bath
Listen to instrumental music
Burning scented candles
Sitting outside the garden
Yoga

To Lift Your Mood
Going to the gym and having a good workout
Spending time with close friends
Having a good telephone chat with mom
Getting an early night's sleep
Watching your favorite comedy shows or YouTube clips
Window shopping

To alleviate boredom

Read a gripping novel
Doing something creative like drawing or rearranging furniture
Socializing
Getting on with household chores
Talking the dog out for a walk in a new place
Surfing the internet for holiday destinations
Exercise
Grocery shopping

To Reward Yourself

Making a nice meal
Baking some cakes
Going to the cinema and having a big bucket of popcorn

To Resist cravings

Doing crosswords
Singing along loudly to music
Going for a long drive in the countryside
Knitting
Mandala Art
Meeting friends or talking to them
Watching T.V.

For Joy & Contentment

Writing a book
Playing with my son/daughter
Going to the spa
Hugging a tree

Drinking Tea / Coffee

Chapter 7

9 Gamut Technique to Reduce Overwhelm Or Resistance

Are you feeling overwhelmed or resisting change? Here is an exciting technique to overcome the overwhelm or resistance in minutes. The 9-gamut procedure involves tapping on a point located on the back of the hand while focusing on the issue and going through 9 steps which involve eye movements, humming and counting. Although initially, it may seem odd, this procedure delivers excellent results. First, locate the point on the back of the hand. It is about an inch down from the knuckles between the little finger and the ring finger. Next, find that space with one or more fingers of the opposite hand, moving from the knuckles toward the wrist until you feel a slight indentation. It feels like the right spot when you gently rub, hold, or tap there. Refer to the hand image to see the location of this point.

You can tap on this point using two or more fingers of the opposite hand. However, I recommend using four fingers for excellent results. The 9-gamut procedure involves tapping on the gamut point while completing nine steps as listed below while you focus on the issue. For each of the nine steps, keep tapping continuously on the gamut spot for approximately 4 to 5 seconds with your head still.

Step 1) Close the eyes.

Step 2) Open the eyes.

Step 3) Keeping your head still, look hard down to your right.

Step 4) Keeping your head still, look hard down to your left.

Step 5) Keeping your head still, roll your eyes in a full circle in one direction.

Step 6) Keeping your head still, roll your eyes in a full circle in the opposite direction.

Step 7) Hum any song out loud for 4 to 5 seconds. You can hum the happy birthday song.

Step 8) Quickly count aloud from 1 to 5 and then from 5 to 1.

Step 9) Hum the song for 4 to 5 seconds.

Even if you interchange the order of the steps when you are doing the gamut tapping, it is fine if you do all the steps. After completing steps 3, 4, 5 and 6, you can allow your eyes to come back into the central/normal position while tapping. I have noticed effective results for my clients using this tip.

9 Gamut Point Location

Want a Demonstration? Click here.

Audio File: 9 Gamut Tapping Demonstration

Play it on speaker for effective results.

Chapter 8

Managing Data & Disturbances

"The key to manage external disturbance is in managing the technology and people that surround you" – Kunal Dudeja

Managing Data & Data Sources

Your calmness depends on the quantum of data you receive and process every day. So, first, review the sources of data that you receive. For example, from T.V., radio, internet, office colleagues, friends, family, emails, boss, team etc. Does all the data that you are receive carry the same level of importance? Do they all need to be processed at the same time when you receive them? Do all of them matter in your life?

For example, you could be talking to a friend who is always complaining in life, you guide him, but he does not listen and keeps complaining. Although you are trying to help them, it could be exhausting. You have chosen to receive the data and information your friend is giving you about his complaints. You are processing it and then providing solutions to your friend. Your processing of data about your friend is in vain as he is only interested in talking about his issue and is unwilling to act on it. Do you want to continue doing that? I guess No. Try and be diplomatic here and avoid being with such friends who drain your energy. You do not want to hurt them. Occasionally listen to them without being mentally fully engaged.

Another example is where you are managing a team of 10 people who are reporting to you. You have a good rapport with all the ten people. However, you find yourself struggling to respond to their queries at times. You do your best, but it stresses you out. Here is what is happening.

- Team member 1 has sent you an email asking for help.
- Team member 2 tried to call you over the phone for something urgent
- Team member 3 is texting you over WhatsApp for an important issue
- Team member 4 is texting you online at work
- Team member 5 has physically come to your cabin to talk
- Team member 6 messaged you over LinkedIn about something

The data sources you are receiving from your team members are many. Setting up a daily meeting of 15-30 minutes with all your team members could save your time. Whether it is daily or your weekly meeting (depending on the industry), the idea is to meet them collectively and knock out all their issues and concerns. Limit the sources of information you receive.

Managing Disturbances

The two aspects which you need to learn to manage external disturbances is technology and people. Learn to quite the technology when you are doing critical tasks. You cannot quite the people around, hence set expectations with them about your time availability. People should know when and how to contact you and when they should not.

Technology Tips

You can turn off your phone's notifications, as it can be distracting. Your messages will still be waiting for you later when you're ready to go through them. Turning your ringer off can also stop each disruption from clogging your mind.

Chapter 9

Surrender & Relax Before Sleeping

Do you need to fight all your battles on your own? What if you could surrender them to someone you trust? Wouldn't that be awesome? Before you go to sleep, write down what is bothering you on a piece of paper. Write whatever comes to your mind. Acknowledge the worries and stresses by writing them down. Once noted, tell your higher power or divine source or someone you believe in to resolve your issues and concerns, and then go to sleep. Surrender to the higher power everything that is bothering you and then sleep peacefully, knowing that it will be taken care of.

Your notes can be as follows.

- *I am worried about getting fired from my job*
- *I am stressed about not losing weight*
- *I am unsure whether my business will do well*
- *Am concerned about the meeting tomorrow*
- *Am not sure how my health will improve*
- *Am tense about my exam tomorrow*
- *Am worried about money*

Its important that you relax your mind and body before your sleep. There are plenty of videos /music you can play of your choice that can help you relax. I would like to suggest this video I found to be helpful for me to relax.

Audio To Relax Your Mind & Body

Chapter 10

Clarity Precedes Calmness

When you cannot take a decision, it can indeed bother you. However, you will be much at peace once you have made up your mind. Make a list of the pros and cons for and against the context of your decision. For example, the pros and cons of going to the party against staying back home. Going out for a walk against watching T.V.
Write the pros and cons on a piece of paper.

For instance, let us assume that you are not happy in your present job. You are unable to decide whether you should change your job. You have been working in this organization for two years. You applied for a new job, and you received the job offer. You are now in a dilemma whether you should accept the job offer or not. Let us see how this technique can help you decide. List down the pros and cons of continuing in the same organization and the pros and cons of joining the new organization.

Pros (For Existing Job)
1) I am in my comfort zone
2) I have acquired all the skills to sustain myself
3) The job is closer to my home

Cons (For Existing Job)
1) I did not receive a good pay rise last year
2) I did not receive appreciation for a project I did successfully
3) The working hours are long

Pros (For New Job)
1) I am getting a 40% pay rise
2) I am getting exciting responsibilities
3) I will get to meet new people

Cons (For New Job)
1) I am not sure whether I can handle more responsibilities
2) I will have to re-build relationships
3) It is far from my home

Here, the decision you will take completely depends on your priorities in life. If your preference is to make more money, then you may decide to take up the new job. However, the new job comes with greater responsibilities, meaning staying back for longer working hours. With the pros of the new job, you should be willing to absorb the cons of the new job too. If your priority is work-life balance, staying back in your current job could make sense as it is closer to your home. You may want to work with your boss and set expectations about your work hours. You may not get 100% of the PIE; however, 30% is still better. You both could agree that you could work lesser hours 2 days a week. That could give you ample time to spend with your family.
In life, we barely get to do the ideal job, where we are comfortable, content, happy, highly remunerating, least

stressful etc. Therefore, you may want to choose those aspects of your job which harmonize with your life priorities and trust yourself to handle challenges.

HALT Your Decision-Making Process

Now that we understand how to make improved decisions with the Pros and Cons technique, I share the HALT technique when you should not take any decision. The HALT is a state of mind where you are likely to make bad decisions. It stands for H- Hungry, A- Agitated, L- Lonely and T-Tired. Please HALT your decision-making process when you are in any of these states. Work on the Pros and cons technique when you are calmer and not in the HALT state.

Chapter 11

Walk A Mile In My Shoes

"What greater thing is there for two human souls than to feel that they are joined for life--to strengthen each other in all labour, to rest on each other in all sorrow, to minister to each other in all pain, to be one with each other in silent unspeakable memories at the moment of the last parting?"— George Eliot.

You can create tremendous peace and calm if you can resolve conflict in the relationships. With the help of this technique, you can gain insights on what you need to do to resolve the dispute and develop an improved understanding with the other person. Whether the other person is your spouse, child, father, mother, boss, colleague, or friend. This technique works. It focuses on answering the below questions

- If you knew from where I came from?
- If you could walk a mile in my shoes?

In this technique, you will think, feel, and hear things from three different perspectives. The different perspectives are – Yourself, the other person, and the observer. Therefore, you will wear the shoes of 3 people (one at a time in your imagination) when you execute this technique.

Step 1) – Sit in a comfortable position with eyes closed. Think of the conflict/argument /fight / heated discussion which happened with this person that is bothering you.

Step 2) Imagine yourself wearing your shoes. Just think of the activating event that created this tension between the two of you. See what you see, hear what you hear, feel what you feel from your perspective. What are you thinking, seeing, hearing, feeling?

Step 3) Open your eyes. Make a note of your thoughts. Then, stand up, sip water.

Step 4) Once again, sit comfortably with your eyes closed. Imagine yourself wearing the shoes of the other person in the same event. Just play the activating event once again. Now try to see what you see from the other person's perspective and hear and feel things from the other person's perspective.

Step 5) Open your eyes. Make a note of your thoughts. Then, stand up, sip water.

Step 6) Once again, sit comfortably with your eyes closed. Imagine yourself wearing the shoes of the observer. Become an observer and play the activating event, which involves you and the other person. See, hear, feel what both of you are seeing, feeling, saying, and doing.

Step 7) Open your eyes. Make a note of your thoughts. Then, stand up, sip water.

Once done, review your thoughts, learnings, and your notes. Then, make a list of actions you will take to create more understanding or reduce conflicts in this relationship.

As an outcome of this activity, you could gain insights as below:

- The tone of my voice can be better
- I can listen before I speak
- The other person did not have any bad intentions. It was a mistake
- We both could act more maturely
- We both are making a mountain of a molehill
- He was not at fault
- I said that because I was angry, I did not mean
- She said that because she was irritated. She generally does not speak that way
- We both need to be more loving and caring towards each other.
- I need to speak with her more respectfully
- She needs to create more understanding towards me
- I need to be more open in this relationship

Once you have identified what action is required to resolve the conflict in the relationship, do not wait. Take the corrective action. Once you have started to take the actions, you will notice that the conflict or the tension between the two of you starts resolving thus creating more peace and calm your overall wellbeing.

PART 2

CALM YOUR MIND AMID CHAOS

Chapter 12

Defining the ABC of Your Problem

"A problem well defined is a problem half-solved" — *John Dewey*

The ABC is a model which breaks down the psychological problem into critical aspects. The A is the activating event, B is the beliefs and thoughts, and C is the consequences. Before we deep dive into the ABC model, let us look at some of the basic terminologies essential for us to proceed further.

Cognitive: Refers to your thoughts, dreams, memories, images, and your focus of attention.

Behavior: Includes everything you do and all the things you choose not to do – such as avoiding situations or sulking instead of speaking.

Therapy: Describes a method of treating a problem – physical, mental, or emotional.

Belief: Refers to your thinking style and your way of understanding the world and your experiences. It also means your rules, values, and general attitude towards living.

Distress: Refers to normal negative human emotion. The intensity of distress is uncomfortable and unpleasant; however, it does not cause long-term problems.

Disturbance: Refers to more extreme, intense negative emotions that can cause long-term problems and interfere significantly in your life.

Consequence: Describes the result or outcome of an event of some kind. In this book, we mainly refer to behavior and emotional consequences

SUDS: SUDS stands for Subjective Unit of Distress Scale. It is a scale used to measure the subjective intensity of distress experienced by an individual about the issue. A score of 0% represents that there is no intensity. A score of 100% means that the issue's intensity is the highest.

Healthy: Refers to appropriate and constructive behavior, thoughts, or emotions.

Unhealthy: Refers to inappropriate and destructive behavior, thoughts, or emotions.

ABC Model of Problem

Now that you are familiar with the basic terms, let us look at the ABC model of a problem.

"A" is the **Activating event.** An activating event means an actual external event, a future event that you anticipate, or an internal event in your mind, such as an image, memory, or even a dream. The 'A' is the activating trigger of our emotional responses. Examples of activating events or activating triggers include:

- You got fired from your job (External Event)
- Your Maths exam date is announced (A Future Event)
- You haven't heard from a friend for longer than usual. (Internal Event)

'B' is representative of your **beliefs and thoughts**. Your beliefs include:

- Your thought patterns and core beliefs.
- Your rules and values
- The demands you make (on yourself, the world, and other people around you).
- The meanings you attach to your life's external and internal events.

'C' stands for the **Consequences**. Consequences include your emotions, behaviors and physical sensations arising from the activating event. Feeling sad, angry, and anxious are emotional consequences. Sulking is a behavioral consequence. Sweaty hands are the physical consequence. Below are some of the examples of ABC

1) ABC of the past event

A – You got fired from your job

B – Belief is that *I am good for nothing,* and thought is that *My boss should not have fired*

C – Emotional consequence is feeling angry (100%) and sad (80%) and the behavioral impact is to sulk.

2) ABC of the future event

A –Math Exams date announced

B – Belief is that *I am bad with Math* and thought is *If I fail, then I will disappoint my parents*

C – Emotional consequence is feeling anxious (80%), and the behavioral outcome is avoiding putting any effort.

3) ABC of internal event

A – Not heard back from a friend for a long time

B – Belief is that *I am not a lovable person* and thought is that *He does not like me anymore*

C – Emotional consequence is feeling sad 100%, and crying is the behavioral consequence.

From the above examples, can we conclude that the activating event is entirely responsible for how you feel and behave? No, not quite.

According to CBT, what determines the quality and intensity of your emotional experience are your thoughts about the event and the meaning you give that event.

For example, if the meaning I give to the internal event of my friend not calling me back as *"He must be busy"* instead of *"He does not like me anymore"*, then the emotion would be concerned and not sad. The behavior would be to call and check on him rather than cry. A change in meaning leads to a change in the emotion and the intensity of the emotion.

Also, it is vital to learn that different people would associate different meanings with similar events. For example, for an activating event, where your friend walks past without acknowledging you, people would give different meanings and experience varied emotions. Also, for the same event you could react differently at different point of time. Let us see an example of this activating event and how different people think, feel, and behave.

Activating Event: Your friend walks past without acknowledging you.

Person 1
Meaning: I must have done something wrong.
Emotion: Anxious
Behavior: Tension in the stomach

Person 2
Meaning: It looks like there is a lot on his mind.
Emotion: Concerned for your friend
Behavior: Relaxed

Person 3
Meaning: He is usually lost and in his zone.
Emotion: Neutral
Behavior: None

Person 4:
Meaning: He does not care about me anymore.
Emotion: Sad
Behavior: Not willing to speak

To summarize, while events are continuously happening in our lives, it is meaning and the beliefs we give to those events that determine how intensely we feel (or don't feel) and how constructively we act (or don't choose to act).

Chapter 13

Basics of Emotional Freedom Technique (EFT) or Tapping

The Emotional Freedom Technique is well known to create effective results since its introduction by Gary Craig in the 1990s. A gentle touch with your fingertips on specific body points, coupled with the power of your intention, can create miraculous results. By the end of this chapter, you will learn the basics of EFT and how to apply EFT to calm your emotions.

What Is EFT or Tapping?

EFT stands for Emotional Freedom Technique, also known as tapping. It is a mind-body technique meant to clear emotional blocks. This technique involves tapping with your fingertips. It is a form of psychological acupressure based on the ancient principle of acupuncture, except that it does not use needles.

EFT combines gentle tapping with your fingertips on key acupuncture points while focusing on the issue. Once you have completed the tapping on the various points, the intensity or the emotional charge of the issue reduces. EFT is easy to understand and apply and very easy to measure the results. This technique was introduced in the 1990s by Gary Craig, and since then, several people worldwide have adopted and embraced EFT. For more information about this technique, please read books written by Gary Craig or visit his website - www.emofree.com.

Location of EFT Tapping Points

Let us understand the location of the EFT tapping points.

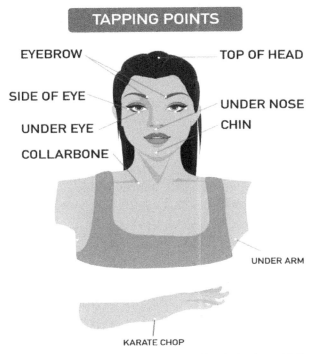

TAPPING POINTS

EYEBROW

TOP OF HEAD

SIDE OF EYE

UNDER NOSE

UNDER EYE

CHIN

COLLARBONE

UNDER ARM

KARATE CHOP

Karate Chop Point (KC): This point is in the middle of the fleshy part of the hand's outside edge. You can tap with four fingers of the opposite hand on this point.

Beginning of Eyebrow (EB): Located at the beginning of the eyebrow, just above and to one side of the nose.

Side of Eye (SE): Located on the outside of the eye socket near the outside corner of the eye.

Under the Eye (UE): Located on the bone underneath the eye, approximately 1 inch below the pupil.

Under Nose (UN): Located between the nose and the upper lip.

Chin (CH): Located between the lower lip and chin.

Collarbone (CB): This point is located on the inner edge of the collarbone. Just an inch or two from the center towards the left or right. This point is where you will feel a slight indentation on your collarbone.

Under Arm (UA): Located at the side of the body. About four inches down from the armpit.

Top of Head (ToH): Located directly in the center on top of the head. When tapping on the top of your head, use all your fingertips.

Tapping with all the Fingers & Thumb (AFT)
Tap using both the hand's fingertips and thumb with each other. In the tapping script, you will see a mention of **AFT** which represents tapping on all fingers & thumbs.

Set-up Statement
A set-up statement is a self-acceptance statement combined with the description of the issue. It typically begins with the words "Even Though", and then the person is supposed to describe the problem and follow it up with an acceptance

statement like "I accept myself" or "I deeply and completely love and accept myself". Examples of some set-up statements for weight loss are:

- Even though I eat because food gives me comfort, I accept myself.
- Even though I have failed many times in my exams, I love and accept myself.
- Even though I have no control over my expenses, I choose to love and accept myself.
- Even though I have a terrible headache, I accept myself
- Even though my financial situation is abysmal, I accept how I feel.

Another variation in the set-up statement is to add a choice statement. Examples of set-up with choice statements are:

- Even though I am stressed, I choose to relax now.
- Even though I cannot control my chocolate craving, I choose to eat consciously.
- Even though losing weight is difficult, I choose to release this perspective now.
- Even though I do not believe in myself, I choose to trust myself
- Even though I do not know how EFT works, I choose to give it a try.

Reminder Phrases
These words or phrases are related to the problem you intend to resolve. Examples of reminder phrases in connection with weight loss could be "It is so difficult to lose weight", "I have tried several times, and I have failed",

"I cannot control my sweet craving", "I do not know how to lose weight" and so on.

Reminder phrases are to be said while tapping on all the points – Karate Chop (KC), Eyebrow (EB), Side of Eye (SE), Under Eye (UE), Under Nose (UN), Chin (CH), Collarbone (CB), Under Arm (UA), All Fingers & Thumb (AFT), and Top of Head (ToH).

Tapping Count and Fingers

Tap 7-8 times on each tapping point using your index, middle and ring finger. You can use a broader coverage for the top of the head, collarbone, and underarm. When you tap, you may be inclined to stay longer on some points, whereas on some, a shorter time.

Tapping Pressure

Tap firmly, but not so hard that you may hurt yourself or leave some bruises. Certainly, tap lightly on the side of the eye and top of the head as those are more delicate parts of the tapping points.

Tapping Ways

You can tap on either side of the body. For example, you could do one round on one side of the body and the other on the other. You could use your left hand to tap or your right hand. You can also use both hands when you tap, except under the nose and on the chin, where there is very little space to tap with both your hands.

Tapping Sequence or Tapping Round
The tapping sequence starts by tapping on the KC and
completes by tapping on the ToH.
Karate Chop (KC)
Eyebrow (EB)
Side of Eye (SE)
Under Eye (UE)
Under Nose (UN)
Chin (CH)
Collarbone (CB)
Under Arm (UA)
AFT (All Fingers & Thumb)
Top of Head (ToH)

Tapping Script
EFT tapping script in this book represents solutions for
resolving the issue. These are general guidelines, and you
are free to modify the script based on your intuition.

Express Gratitude
Once your tapping is complete, express gratitude to the EFT
technique, yourself, and anyone else you would like to.

Close the Session
Once you have expressed gratitude, you may choose to write
notes about corrective actions you want to take after the
session, and any learning outcomes and realizations.

What to Expect Post Tapping
You may feel drowsy, thirsty, sleepy, fresh, tired, crying,
sad, energetic, yawning, burping, wanting to use the

washroom. These are all signs of release and the shifts happening post tapping. Side effects of tapping are that you could feel a sense of ease, a sense of freedom. You could feel happy and delighted too.

EFT Tapping Methods
There are two methods of tapping:

Method 1 – Talk, Feel and Tap Method
While you are tapping on the points, talk out loud about the issue you are facing. Talk as if you are expressing your problem to your friend. When you do this, you will be surprised how hidden emotions come up for tapping. This method is known as the "Tell the Story Method". It is like talking about your issue in the form of a story.

Method 2 – Think, Feel and Tap Method
As the name suggests, keep tapping while thinking about your problem. Think about the event or the person that has caused this issue. See what you see, hear what you hear and feel the emotions. Play the issue like a movie in your mind and keep tapping on the points. You can use this method when you do not wish to talk about your issue.

If your issue's intensity is exceptionally high, you may want to speak to your therapist.

Guidelines for Effective Tapping

1. Do not generalize your issue. Be specific about your issue.

2. When you tap, turn off or put your phone or put it on silent mode.

3. Wear comfortable clothes and find a relaxing place.

4. Remove any item that may hinder tapping, such as your eyeglasses, rings, or bracelets.

5. Drink water in between the tapping rounds.

Chapter 14

Calming Emotions For a Single Issue

Now that you know your ABC let us learn to tap on it.
Tapping comprises of three rounds - Rounds 1 and 2, you
tap on all the body points and talk about your A, B and C.
The intent is to reduce the emotional intensity of your issue.
Then, in round 3, you tap to gain more control over your
emotions.

Reduce the Emotional Intensity (Rounds 1 and 2)

While tapping on the points, talk out loud about your A, B
and C. Go all out and release the steam of emotions. Talk as
if you are expressing your issue to your close friend.
Describe the problem and what is bothering you. The key
here is to talk intuitively about your issue and as naturally as
possible. Do not put any effort into thinking. You won't get
this wrong. Do two rounds of tapping.

Gain Emotional Control (Round 3)

Once you have let off the steam of unhealthy emotions, the
next step is to take charge of your feelings. Tap on each
point, saying out loud the set-up statement. This statement
structure as explained earlier starts with the "Even Though"
followed by the single statement that entirely describes your
issue. It is followed by the acceptance and love statement or
the choice statement, i.e. I accept and love myself. Below
are examples of explaining your problem in a single
statement:

- I felt hurt by the way he spoke to me
- I am feeling guilty because I could not speak with her
- Am furious with the efforts he put into the presentation
- Am nervous about my exams
- Am feeling anxious about that meeting
- She should not have done that

Examples of love and acceptance and choice statements are as below:
- I accept myself
- I accept myself and my situation
- I love and accept myself
- I love myself
- I accept how I feel
- I accept myself and choose to relax now
- I choose to relax now
- I choose to stay calm
- I choose to heal
- I accept myself and the other person
- I accept myself and other person anyway
- I choose to relax
- I accept my feelings and relax now
- I forgive myself
- I accept and forgive myself
- I accept and forgive myself and others

Once you have created the set-up statement, say it aloud while tapping on all the body points - from Karate Chop to Top of Head. The structure will be Even though, <Tell the

single statement describing your issue>, I <Tell your acceptance or choice statement>. Examples as below

- Even though I felt hurt by the way he spoke to me, I love and accept myself
- Even though I felt guilty because I could not speak with her, I accept myself
- Even though I am furious with the efforts he put into the presentation, I choose to relax now
- Even though I am nervous about my exams, I accept how I feel
- Even though I am feeling anxious about that meeting, I accept and trust myself.
- Even though I believe that she should not have done that, I choose to forgive her.

ILLUSTRATION

(A) Activating Event: John spoke with me very rudely
(B) Beliefs & Thoughts: He should not have spoken in such a rude way.
(C) Emotional Consequence: I am feeling Angry & Sad
(C) Behavioural Consequence: I am not willing to talk to him

Rounds 1 (Reduce the Emotional Intensity)
KC: I cannot believe the way John spoke with me
EB: Why did he talk with me this way?
SE: We are best friends. How dare he speak so rudely
UE: I have never talked to him like that
UN: I am very angry with the way he reacted

CH: I am feeling very hurt and sad
CB: How dare he speak to me this way
UA: I hate John
AFT: I am not going to talk to him
ToH: He better understands his mistake and apologizes

Rounds 2 (Reduce the Emotional Intensity)

KC: I'm so angry at him
EB: I never expected this behaviour from him
SE: He has created a dent in our friendship
UE: I am so upset
UN: I treated him as a family friend
CH: I am deeply hurt
CB: He should not have spoken with me like this
UA: I so dislike him
AFT: I do not think he deserves my friendship
ToH: I am so sad

Round 3 (Gain Emotional Control)

The one line which entirely describes the issue is "Am angry because John spoke rudely". The Love and acceptance statement could be I accept and love myself.

KC: Even though I am angry because John spoke rudely, I accept and love myself.
EB: Even though I am angry because John spoke rudely, I accept and love myself.
SE: Even though I am angry because John spoke rudely, I accept and love myself.
UE: Even though I am angry because John spoke rudely, I accept and love myself.

59

UN: Even though I am angry because John spoke rudely, I accept and love myself.

CH: Even though I am angry because John spoke rudely, I accept and love myself.

CB: Even though I am angry because John spoke rudely, I accept and love myself.

UA: Even though I am angry because John spoke rudely, I accept and love myself.

AFT: Even though I am angry because John spoke rudely, I accept and love myself.

ToH: Even though I am angry because John spoke rudely, I accept and love myself.

To summarize, tap on the ABC for rounds 1 and 2.

Round 3 tap entirely with the set-up statement.

Please Note: This is only a suggestive way to do the tapping. If you are an EFT practitioner and you want to do the tapping the way you have learned, you are free to do so :-)

Chapter 15

Calm Your Emotions
For Multiple Issues

You may get overwhelmed with too many things happening around you, or there could also be times when you are doing nothing but thinking about multiple issues. It is essential to your emotions when you are in such a situation. You can do tapping by saying out loud *"Everything that is bothering me now.* You may choose to change the script according to your situation. Some other examples are as below.

- Everything and everybody stressing me today
- Everybody irritating me now
- This situation
- This situation at work & home is bothering me now
- Everything about my work is bothering me now.
- Everything about my spouse worrying me etc.

Once you feel the SUDS score has reduced considerably, you may want to start tapping on a specific issue bothering you the most out of the multiple problems. Refer to the previous chapter on Calming the Emotional Intensity of Your Specific Issue. Below is the tapping script for calming your emotions when there are multiple issues.

Round 1
KC: Everything that is bothering me now. Everything that is bothering me now. Everything that is bothering me now.

EB: Everything that is bothering me now. Everything that is bothering me now. Everything that is bothering me now.
SE: Everything that is bothering me now. Everything that is bothering me now. Everything that is bothering me now.
UE: Everything that is bothering me now. Everything that is bothering me now. Everything that is bothering me now.
UN: Everything that is bothering me now. Everything that is bothering me now. Everything that is bothering me now.
CH: Everything that is bothering me now. Everything that is bothering me now. Everything that is bothering me now.
CB: Everything that is bothering me now. Everything that is bothering me now. Everything that is bothering me now.
UA: Everything that is bothering me now. Everything that is bothering me now. Everything that is bothering me now.
AFT: Everything that is bothering me now. Everything that is bothering me now. Everything that is bothering me now.
ToH: Everything that is bothering me now. Everything that is bothering me now. Everything that is bothering me now.

To Tap along with me. Click here.

Calming Emotions For Multiple Issues

(Play it on speaker for effective results)

Chapter 16

Calming Emotions When
You cannot name the Feeling

At times you may feel mixed emotions. For example, you could be feeling sad, angry, and guilty. If the emotional intensity is very high, you may want to talk to your therapist. However, the below tapping sequence could help calm those emotions when the emotional intensity is not very high.

Round 1
KC: This emotion. This emotion. This emotion.
EB: This emotion. This emotion. This emotion.
SE: This emotion. This emotion. This emotion.
UE: This emotion. This emotion. This emotion.
UN: This emotion. This emotion. This emotion.
CH: This emotion. This emotion. This emotion.
CB: This emotion. This emotion. This emotion.
UA: This emotion. This emotion. This emotion.
AFT: This emotion. This emotion. This emotion.
ToH: This emotion. This emotion. This emotion.

As needed, do more rounds of tapping. Once your emotions are calm, you can then look at the specific issue bothering you and then do the taping, as explained earlier in chapter.

Need a buddy to help? Click here

Audio File: Calming Emotions When You Cannot Name The Feeling

(Play it on speaker for effective results)

Chapter 17

Basics of Cognitive Behavioral Therapy

What is CBT?

Dr Aaron T. Beck pioneered CBT in the 1960s. Cognitive Behavioral Therapy (CBT) is an action-oriented form of psychological treatment practiced by thousands of therapists worldwide. **CBT helps individuals understand the connection between their thoughts and feelings and how their thoughts and feelings influence their behavior. When people change their thoughts, they will also change their emotions and behavior.**

Thousands of research trials have demonstrated that CBT is an effective treatment for anxiety and depression. Moreover, it is helpful across the lifespan – children, adolescents, adults, and older adults can all benefit.

Definition of CBT

As defined by the American Psychiatric Association – Cognitive behavioral therapy (CBT) helps people identify and change thinking and behavior patterns that are harmful or ineffective, replacing them with more accurate thoughts and functional behaviors. It can help a person focus on current problems and how to solve them. It often involves practicing new skills in the real world.

Key Characteristics of CBT

- Emphasizes the role of the personal meanings you give to events in determining your emotions and behaviours.
- Focuses more on how your thoughts/beliefs are managed rather than the root cause of the issue.
- Can address emotional issues from the past, present & future by creating linkages on how they impact your thoughts, feelings, and behaviors.
- Strives to normalize and regulate your emotions, physical sensations, and thinking.

Characteristics of Human Beings

- We experience life with our senses, seeing, hearing, listening, touching, feeling, smelling. We are processors of our experience and not victims of circumstances.
- We do not need to be fixed. Instead, be heard well and understood.
- As we learn unhelpful ways of thinking, we can also unlearn them.
- We also can choose a new set of habits, thought patterns and behaviours.
- We are solely responsible for what we think, feel, and do.
- We cannot control thoughts entering our minds, but we can choose to act or ignore them.
- We must become better versions of ourselves rather than just feeling better.

Characteristics of Thoughts

It is vital to understand the below characteristics of thoughts
- Thoughts are not facts.
- Thoughts are mental events taking place in our minds.
- They may or may not be true.
- They may or may not be helpful.
- We do not have to respond to all of them. We can choose to ignore some.
- Thoughts include beliefs, attitudes, assumptions, and images.
- Unpleasant thoughts/memories could create unpleasant emotions.
- Pleasant thoughts/memories could create pleasant emotions.

NAT (Negative Automatic Thoughts)

Negative automatic thoughts are thoughts that seem to pop into your head without any warning sign or welcome. That's why we refer to these thoughts as automatic or intuitive. When an event happens in your life, it triggers thoughts. Some of them could be healthy or unhealthy. For example, you ordered Pizza in a restaurant. The waiter bought you a burger and quickly left. What is the first thought you get after this event?

- *What the hell just happened?*
- *Where is my Pizza?*
- *Why did he serve me a burger?*
- *Did he mistakenly do so?*
- *That's Great! I so wanted to eat a burger.*

After this event of the waiter serving you a burger instead of a pizza, you could experience NAT – Negative Automatic Thoughts if you want to eat the Pizza or PAT – Positive Automatic Thoughts if you are happy to eat the burger.

Another example is when you are in a deep sleep. Around 2.00 AM, you get a call from a family relative. This family relative does not usually call you late at night. Your immediate thought could be:

- What has happened?
- Are they safe?
- Is there any medical emergency?
- Is he calling me by mistake?
- Hope all is well.

Noticing your NATs can increase your chances of managing your emotions by allowing you to correct any unhelpful thoughts you may be having about an event.

The Cognitive Triangle
As per CBT, our thoughts, behaviors, and emotions are linked and affect each other. Therefore, the three components of the cognitive triangle are:

Thoughts: What we think affects the way we feel and act.

Behavior: What we do effects affects how we think and feel.

Emotions: What we feel affects what we think and do.

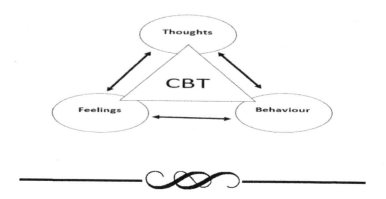

Chapter 18

Understanding Thinking Errors

Unwelcoming NATs are thinking errors that trigger unhealthy emotions and behaviors. Once we learn these thinking errors, it is vital to acknowledge and drop them. Events from the past, present or future can trigger these NATs and thinking errors.

Thinking Error # 1 - Black & White

The All or Nothing or Black and White is extreme thinking which causes you to experience intense emotions. It makes you think and behave in extremes leaving no room for exceptions. You often think of words like - *Impossible, Never, Always, completely, Perfect, either this or that, either good or bad.* You either love someone entirely or hate them completely. You think to achieve grand success or be a complete disaster, be a sinner or a saint, work with 100% commitment or don't work at all. For example, you have started going to the gym and following a good diet to lose weight. However, you cave into the temptation of chocolate. Since your thinking is Black and White, you think that your diet has gone for a toss, and you eat the complete box of chocolates.

Catch hold of yourself when you think in the extreme. You are a human and bound to make mistakes. Mentally allow and accept two seemingly opposite thoughts or choices. To overcome this thinking, ask yourself questions such as

- Am I thinking in the extreme?
- Do I see any all or nothing thought pattern?
- Are there any grey areas that I can consider?

If you are one of those who fall in this category, I suggest that you stop reading any further for a week. Just keep asking the above questions to yourself through out the week. Ask these questions to yourself every 2-3 hours in the day. Notice and correct your thinking. Once you have corrected your thinking for a week (or more as the case may be) come back and continue reading further. Follow this solution if you fall in other thinking error category.

Thinking Error # 2 - MAXIMIZATION or MINIMIZATION

Maximization: It is also called Catastrophizing, and to describe it is making a mountain out of a molehill. We take a minor adverse event and blow it out of proportion by imagining all sorts of disasters resulting from that one single event. You assume the worst-case scenario and jump to the worst possible conclusion. Assuming an accident for late arrival, a break-up for a minor argument, or a job loss when you receive a little push from your boss are all examples of catastrophic thinking. People with this thinking error think such as:

- As he has not reached home yet, something terrible must have happened to him
- My nose is so big that no one will love me.

To de-catastrophize this thinking, you can ask questions as below.

- Am I catastrophizing this thought?
- Am I blowing this out of proportion?

Minimization: Minimization is the opposite of Maximization. In this type of thinking, you give less importance to things than they deserve. For example, not wearing your seat belt while driving with the thought that *"I am a very safe driver, and nothing will happen to me"* is a case of Minimization.

Thinking Error # 3 - DEMANDING

You think words – *Should have, should be, he should, I should, I must, he must, need, ought, got to.* This type of thinking implies placing a demand on yourself or the people around you. It makes your thinking rigid, allowing less scope for flexibility or exceptions. Some examples of Demanding thinking errors are:

- *Since I am kind to you, you should also be kind to me.*
- *I must always be perfect*
- *I should never be anxious*
- *People should respect me*
- *She should not have said that*

Ask yourself the below question to identify this thinking error: Am I using words like 'should', 'must', 'ought', and 'have to' to make rigid rules about myself, the world, or other people?

Please note that these are rigid expectations about you and others related to thoughts, behaviors, and actions. *I should study to pass the exam, I should go to then dentist to fix my tooth, I should be conscious about expenses to save more* are examples of tasks and activities. These do not fall in the demanding thinking error.

Thinking Error # 4 - PERSONALIZATION

You take it personally and ignore the facts about the event or situation. You consider yourself fully responsible for an adverse event you were not primarily responsible for. When you do this, you feel unnecessarily guilty or hurt.

- *My mother is not happy. It must be because of me.*
- *We lost the game because I did not do well.*

For example, as a therapist, you ask your client to do some assignments before meeting in the next session. When you met your client, he mentioned he had not done his homework. You then start feeling guilty with the thought that "I cannot help my client".

It is important to consider the facts and your own responsibilities. You cannot be responsible for everything and everyone. If you think you are, then it is this personalization error.

Thinking Error # 5 - JUMPING TO CONCLUSIONS

There are two ways you could be jumping to conclusions. Either by doing Fortune Telling or by Mind Reading. Let us look at them in detail:

74

Fortune Telling: In this type of thinking, you have already predicted negative results. You have concluded that things will not happen as you expect them to happen. For example, thoughts like *"I know I will not get the job"*, *"I will not enter a relationship with Patricia as I know it won't work"*, or *"I won't start my business as I know it won't work"*.

Mind Reading: You assume what the other person thinks or feels about you. For example, not talking to your boss about your promotion, assuming that he will not promote you. Likewise, not eating lunch alone in the cafeteria as other people would think you are a lonely loser.

In small doses, mind reading can be a helpful tool. Certain nonverbal behaviours and verbal reactions can hint at what someone is thinking. For instance, when we tell someone something and their jaw drops, we assume the other person is surprised. This kind of mind-reading is helpful and not an example of a thinking error. However, when used too much or without much evidence, mind reading can be problematic.

Ask yourself the below questions to get out of this thinking error trap.

- Am I predicting the future instead of waiting to see what happens? (Fortune-telling)
- Am I jumping to a conclusion about what people are thinking about me? (Mind reading)

Thinking Error # 6 - EMOTIONAL REASONING

As the name suggests, you give reasons and apply logic based on your feelings and emotions. Your emotions influence how you think and act. You feel sad, hence you believe that your job is not good. You feel guilty. Hence you think you must have hurt someone else. You feel sad, and hence you think that your relationship is not good. You feel low in confidence; hence you think you cannot pass the test.

While your emotions can give you hints about what is happening in your life, it is not the only indicator. This thinking error assumes that your feelings influence all your thoughts and actions. Emotional thinking errors are thoughts such as –

- I feel guilty; hence I must have done something terrible.
- I am not feeling good today; hence it's a bad day
- I am a failure because I feel like a failure

Emotional Reasoning also creates procrastination tendencies. For example, you avoid cleaning your wardrobe because you feel there is way too much to clean, and it will take a lot of your time and energy. As a result, you procrastinate for months. Then, one day when you decide and clean your wardrobe, you realize how easy it was and feel happy about it.

Thinking Error # 7 - OVER GENERALIZATION

Overgeneralizing is the error of drawing global conclusions from one or more negative events. When you find yourself thinking words like *'always'*, *'never'*, *'people are . . .'*, or

76

'the world's is ...', you may be overgeneralizing. Some of the errors include -

- People cannot be trusted because once someone broke my trust
- I will never be able to speak in public because I once had a panic attack before giving a speech.
- I will never sit on a horse again as once I sat and I had a fall

Let us understand this error with an example. You enter the conference room 5 minutes late for an important meeting. You think that "I am always late for important meetings". Factually speaking, of the hundreds of conferences you may have attended, you were late only for three of them. However, the thinking error "Overgeneralization" does not let you examine this fact. Instead, it makes you feel guilty that you are always late. In the next chapter I explain about acknowledging and dropping this thinking errors. For now, learn and absorb them.

Thinking Error # 8 - LABELLING
Here you assign a negative label to yourself or the other person. It is a thinking error that could originate from a single adverse event. It takes the form of "Because I did X, I am Y", Because he did X, he is Y.

- I lost the game, so I am a loser.
- Because I forgot to call my mom, I am a terrible daughter.
- He cried while watching that movie; he must be a cry-baby.

- I lost my keys; hence I am irresponsible!
- I could not spend time with my daughter this entire week. I am a bad father.
- My son fell while he was playing in the garden. I am an irresponsible mother.

To overcome this error, ask yourself, "So What".

- So, what if I lost the game, it does not make me a loser.
- So, what if I forgot to call mom. I usually do call her. It does not make me a terrible daughter.
- So what, I could not spend time with my daughter this week. I will do so next week. It does not make me a bad father.
- So what if my son fell and got a slight bruise. It is okay. It does not make me an irresponsible mom.

The more labels your drop from yourself and others, the calmer your thoughts will become and thereby your life.

Thinking Error # 9 - MENTAL FILTERING

In this thinking, you tend to focus only on the negative. For example, suppose you have a negative view about yourself (such as I am not good enough) about the world (the world is bad) and about others (I cannot trust people). In that case, you could filter out things and accept only those conversations/ thoughts which match your negative beliefs. For example, let us assume your core belief is "I am a failure". Here is the situation-You delivered an excellent presentation to the board of directors of your organization. Your presentation went excellent. However, there was a spelling mistake in your presentation. Someone brought this to your attention during the presentation. You will ignore that the board appreciated your presentation because your mental filter will only absorb the spelling mistake. The spelling error gets focused as it is in sync with your core belief of "I am a failure". Although your presentation was a success, in your view, it was a failure because of this mental filter.

Thinking Error # 10 - DISCOUNTING THE POSITIVE
This thinking error implies discounting the good things that have happened to you—discounting your positives, creations, and efforts you would have taken for yourself or others.

In this thinking, you undervalue your positives, capability, and talents. You discount the positive results you have achieved. For example, you got a promotion in your ob. You were the only one who got promoted in your department. You think, "That's a fluke" or "I got lucky". You have discounted the efforts you put in to get the promotion. Similarly, you have lost weight. Your friend praises you that you are looking fantastic. You tell your friend, "I only lost 10 pounds. I am the same". You have entirely discounted the compliment your friend gave you. Instead of saying "Thank you" and acknowledging the compliment and receiving the appreciation, you ignored the efforts you put to lose those 10 pounds.

Thinking Error # 11 - LOW TOLERANCE TO FRUSTRATION or BOREDOM
Some people cannot tolerate frustration or boredom. They are likely to assume that something challenging to endure is intolerable. This thinking error magnifies the discomfort in

achieving goals. One may tend to quit or procrastinate the task, thinking that it is too dull or frustrating. Also, they underestimate the ability to cope with discomfort. For example, you want to lose weight and start walking on the treadmill. You do it for 3-4 days, and then you get bored. You then decide to walk early morning instead. You experience discomfort waking up early morning and then decide not to pursue your weight loss goal. The boredom to walk on the treadmill and the discomfort of waking up early morning resulted to quit your weight loss goal. Most of the time, things are not served on your platter to enjoy. You have got to put in the hard work to achieve something. Learn to distinguish between things becoming difficult vs unbearable and boring vs intolerable. Push yourself to do the tasks even if they give you discomfort in the short term, as they are likely to provide you with comfort/ contentment/ happiness in the long term. The key is to take baby steps. Identify the minor physical action you can take today to make a 0.1% progress towards your goal.

Chapter 19

Identify & Acknowledge
Thinking Errors

The trigger to identify thinking errors is your emotional or behavioral consequence. For example, when your emotions are low/ unhappy/ unhealthy, that is the right time to recognize and acknowledge thinking errors.

When your get a NAT, ask the below questions

Identifying Thinking Errors

1. Am I catastrophizing this thought by giving it too much importance? (Maximization)
2. Am I jumping to the worst possible conclusion? (Maximization)
3. Am I thinking in the extreme/all or nothing? (Black or White)
4. Am I using words like 'should', 'must', 'ought', and 'have to' to make rigid rules about myself, the world, or other people? (Demanding)
5. Am I getting carried away by my emotions instead of considering facts? (Emotional Reasoning)
6. Am I taking an event or someone's behavior too personally or blaming myself and overlooking other factors? (Personalizing)
7. Am I labelling myself or others as a failure, unlovable, useless? (Labelling)

8. Am I using words like 'always' and 'never' to draw generalized conclusions from a specific event? (Overgeneralizing)
9. Am I predicting the future instead of waiting to see what happens? (Fortune-telling)
10. Am I jumping to conclusions about what people are thinking about me? (Mind reading)
11. Am I focusing only on the negative and overlooking the positive? (Mental filtering)
12. Am I discounting positive information or twisting a positive into a negative? (Discounting the positive)
13. Am I quitting or withdrawing myself, considering this is unbearable and intolerable?

Acknowledge Thinking Errors

Once you have identified the thinking error (say Demanding), you must acknowledge and drop this thinking error. Work on 1 thinking error every week to make good progress.

Some examples include as below.

Thought: She is always late hence irresponsible
Acknowledgement: I acknowledge that I was labelling her as irresponsible, and I now choose to be more aware of my thinking.

Thought: My boss will never promote me
Acknowledgement: I acknowledge that I was mind reading and jumping to conclusions. I now choose to think of possibilities.

Thought: I got promoted by fluke.
Acknowledgement: I acknowledge that I was discounting my hard work

Thought: He is either my best friend or my worst enemy
Acknowledgement: I acknowledge black and white thinking.
Thought: She is always late
Acknowledgement: I acknowledge that I was over-generalizing as she is usually on time.

Thought: I am feeling guilty as I forgot to wish on his birthday
Acknowledgement: I acknowledge that I was personalizing and chose to go easy with myself.

Thought: My boss will fire me as he gave me feedback
Acknowledgement: I acknowledge catastrophizing, black and white thinking and jumping to conclusions about my boss's feedback.

Thought: I am a bad father
Acknowledgement: I acknowledge that I was labelling myself, and I dropped this label now.

When your feel low / unhappy / unhealthy due to an external event, notice your NAT. Ask the thinking error questions and drop the thinking error. You need not always know which type of thinking error it is. If you know that there is a thinking mistake, it is good enough for you to acknowledge it and drop that thinking. Just say that "I acknowledge there was a thinking error and I drop this thought now".

Chapter 20

EFT + CBT Model for Absolute Calmness

"The happiness of your life depends upon the quality of your thoughts: therefore, guard accordingly, and take care that you entertain no notions unsuitable to virtue and reasonable nature."— *Marcus Aurelius*

Up until now, we have understood the basics of EFT and CBT. We will combine the power of both therapies to get better at managing our emotions & thoughts. You can use the EFT+CBT model for past events, present situations, and future uncertain events. Knowing this one model can help you find calm for most of the things and situations in your life. This model can be applied to be calm for almost everything. I use the word *almost everything* to exclude those situations where you would need to consult your therapist and cannot do it on your own. The faster you heal your emotions and correct your thinking, with the help of this model, the quicker you become calm and at peace.

This complete model is divided into three stages: Let us look at each stage in detail:

Stage 1 – Calm Your Emotions:

Calm your emotions with tapping or by any other method you feel right. Refer the earlier chapter on Calming emotions for specific issue or multiple issues. To give you a summary of what you need to do as step 1 is - Tap for two rounds on your ABC. For the third round, create a one-line statement describing your issue and tap on all the body points saying – Even Though <Followed by the one line which entirely describes your problem> and then tell the Acceptance/Love statement or the choice statement.

Stage 2 –Correct Your Thought:
This stage is further divided into 5 steps as below. We will look at each step-in detail.

- Pen down your belief or thought
- Acknowledge the thinking error
- Dilute the old Thought
- Create a New healthy thought
- Imbibe the new healthy thought

Pen Down Your Thought or Belief
Pin down Your B (Beliefs & Negative Automatic Thoughts). Make a note (mental or on paper) of the NAT / Belief arising out of the activating event. Examples of NATs or belief is as follow:

- He should respect me
- He always lies
- I am good for nothing
- I will not be able to pass the Math exams
- I am not a good father
- I am a failure
- She should not have said that
- She is ignoring me

85

- She is always late
- My boss will never promote me
- I am bad at managing money
- It is all my fault
- I should have known this earlier
- They all think bad about me
- I have completely messed it up
- I am good for nothing
- I am not lovable
- How could he say that to me?
- Why did they behave the way they did?

If your thought is in the form of a question, then convert your thinking into a statement. Example How could he say that to me? would be "He should not have said that". Or why did they behave the way they did? would be "They should not have behaved the way they did.".

Identify & Acknowledge Thinking Errors

Once you have noted your thought, ask questions to identify which thinking error applies to your thought. Essentially, if you have learned and understood the thinking errors well, you can quickly identify the thinking error. However, if you are still learning about it, you can ask the thinking error questions. Refer chapter on Identifying & Acknowledging thinking errors.

Learn, practice and you get more comfortable in catching your thinking error within your NAT.

Diluting the Old Thought

Once you have identified and acknowledged the thinking error, the thought starts losing its intensity. You can ask the below questions to further dilute your thought:

- Would I encourage my loved one to think this way?
- Is my thought logical, or is it based on my feelings?
- Do I have evidence to prove that this thought is 100% true?
- If I continue to think this way for the next 5 hours, how likely I am to feel better or take any progressive action?
- What am I missing out on thinking this way?
- What costs am I paying to think this way? Is it worth thinking this way?
- Is my thought extreme or rigid?
- Am I overestimating the impact of this thought on myself or another person?
- Am I underestimating my ability to cope if this thought is true?
- Does this thought hold any significance when I look at the larger picture of my (or other person's) life?
- Would this thinking matter a year from now?
- Is this thinking helping me to progress toward my life goals?
- What would I see, hear, or feel about the event if I were in the other person's shoes?
- If the other person was in my shoes, what would they see, hear, or feel about the event?

Once done, reassess your SUDS score and make a note of it. You may not necessarily ask all the above questions to dilute your thought. Asking 3-4 questions may be good enough. You will become better and quickly know which question you need to ask with continuous practice. Also, with different situations and emotions, all these questions would carry different importance. I love the below questions. It gives me excellent and quick results. However, you can go by what works for you:

- Would I encourage my loved one to think this way?
- If I continue to think this way for the next 5 hours, how likely I am to feel better or take any progressive action?
- What costs I am paying to think this way? Is it worth thinking this way?
- Is this thinking helping me to progress toward my life goals?

Create New Healthy Thought
Once the old thought gets diluted, the next step is to create a new healthy view. Asking the below questions would help you replace the old thought with the new one:
- Is there another way of looking at this situation?
- How would I need to change my thought to feel better and act more constructively?
- How differently would I think ten years from now?
- What is a different thought I would suggest to my loved ones if they were in my situation?

Make a note of your new healthy thought. Here are examples of the new healthy thought against the old thinking.

Old Thought: He should respect me
New Thought: I prefer he gives me respect. I am okay if he does not.

Old Thought: I will not be able to pass the Math exams
New Thought: I can try my best

Old Thought: I am not a good father I have made mistakes
New Thought: I have made mistakes but that does not mean I am not a good father. I can work towards becoming a better father.

Old Thought: I am a failure
New Thought: I am not a total failure. I have achieved success in a few areas.

Old Thought: She should not have said that
New Thought: I prefer she did not say that.

Old Thought: She is ignoring me
New Thought: She would be busy. I will talk to her and check.

Old Thought: He is always late
New Thought: He got a late couple of times, and that's okay

Old Thought: My boss will never promote me
New Thought: My boss may or may not promote me. I will talk to my boss and find out.

Old Thought: I am bad at managing money
New Thought: I am learning money management.

Old Thought: It is all my fault
New Thought: I learned it now. I will be aware in the future.

Old Thought: I should have known this earlier
New Thought: I could not have known this. Had I known, my action/behavior would be different.

Old Thought: They all think bad about me
New Thought: I do not know what they think about me

Old Thought: I have completely messed it up
New Thought: I got it wrong this time around. I am learning from my mistake. It's okay for me to make mistakes.

Old Thought: How could he say that to me?
New Thought: I prefer he did not say that.

Old Thought: Why did they behave the way they did?
New Thought: I wish they did not behave the way they did.

Imbibing Your New Healthy Thought

Keep your hands on your heart and say out loud the new healthy thought 5-6 times with the intent to imbibe it in your conscious and subconscious mind. Once done, reassess your SUDS score.

Stage 3 – Take Corrective Action

After correcting the emotions & thoughts, sometimes there could be scenarios where you need to act. Actions like talking and clarifying your stand, apologizing to someone, going for a vacation, forgiving yourself, and forgiving another person. You can ask yourself the below questions

- What constructive action is needed now?
- What can I do to heal this?
- What can I say to the other person?
- What action is required so that I do not feel the same way in future?

Summarizing the Complete Method of EFT+CBT

Stage 1 Calming Emotions

Step 1 – Tapping on your ABC
Step 2 – Tapping on your ABC
Step 3 – Tap on the set-up statement

Stage 2 – Correcting Thinking

Step 4 – Pen down your belief or thought
Step 5 – Acknowledge the thinking error
Step 6 – Dilute the old Thought
Step 7 – Create a New healthy thought
Step 8 – Imbibe the new healthy thought

Stage 3 – Taking Corrective Action

Step 9 – Take corrective action

PLEASE NOTE:

1. I have suggested EFT for calming your emotions. If you want to use any other method from this book (or from elsewhere), you are free to use that if you can calm your emotions. Depending on the emotional intensity, you can entirely skip stage 1 and move to stage 2.

2. You may not necessarily ask all the thinking error questions each time. However, once you understand the concept, you can directly acknowledge the thinking error and move further.

3. You need not ask all thought diluting questions either. Instead, you can refer to those questions as a reference. Once you become comfortable, you could ask a few questions and weaken the thought.

4. You can directly jump to step 7 of creating the new healthy thought and immediately notice the change in your emotions.

5. The model is suggestive only. Please consult your therapist if your emotional intensity is high.

You can feel free to reach us at www.kunaldudeja.com where we conduct training to help your community, college, or organization to explain this model.

I have created this cheat sheet that has all the questions as follows. You can take a picture of this page and put it on your phone if you wish to refer to this page. Take a printout and put it in front of your desk.

EFT+ CBT Model for Absolute Calmness (Cheat Sheet)

Steps 1 & 2 – Tap on your ABC
Step 4 – Pen the Belief/Thought
Step 6 – Dilute the Old thought
Step 8 – Imbibe Healthy Thought

Step 3 – Tap on the Set-up
Step 5 – Spot Thinking Error
Step 7 – Create New Thought
Step 9 – Take corrective   Action

Thinking Error Questions

Am I catastrophizing this thought?
Am I thinking in black or white?
Am I emotional reasoning?
Am I labelling myself or others?
Am I predicting the future?
Am I focusing only on negative?
Is it frustrating or unbearable?

Jumping to a conclusion?
Am I demanding/ should be?
Am I personalizing?
Am I over-generalizing?
Am I mind reading?
Discounting the positive?
Is it boring or unbearable?

Thought Diluting Questions

Would I encourage my loved one to think this way?
Is my thought logical, or is it based on my feelings?
Do I have evidence to prove that this thought is 100% true?
If I continue to think this way for the next 5 hours, how likely I am to feel better or take any progressive action?
What am I missing out on thinking this way?
What costs am I paying to think this way? Is it worth it?
Is my thought extreme or rigid?
Am I overestimating the impact of this thought on myself/others?
Am I underestimating my ability to cope if this thought is true?
Does this thought hold importance in the larger picture of life?
Would this thinking matter a year from now?
Is this thinking helping me to progress toward my life goals?
What would I see, hear, or feel about the event in the other person's shoes?
If the other person was in my shoes, what would they see, hear, feel?

New Healthy Thought Creating Questions

Is there another way of looking at this situation?
How would I need to change my thought to feel better and act?
What is a different thought I would suggest to my loved one?
How differently would I think ten years from now?

Corrective Action Related Questions

What can I do to heal this? What can I say to the other person?
What constructive action is needed?
What action is required so that I do not feel the same way in future?

Client's Speak

"Thank you so much, Kunal. I believe that God sent you into my life because HE was aware that I'd need someone to guide me in managing my emotions. After CBT and EFT, my perception has changed. Even under stress, I can look at the situation from a different point of view which is empowering. The entire process of analysing my situation, thoughts and emotions has helped me identify the error in my thought process. It has also obliged to accept it and replace it with a more empowering view. Thank you so much, Kunal. Keep healing people" - Grateful Client.

"Thank you, Kunal. These three days have been reflective for me. I have started to recognize my thinking errors and have learned to drop away from the thoughts that don't serve me. The EFT works on my emotional triggers. I feel that after this session, I will be able to manage my emotions and thoughts better" - Grateful Client

"I have been carrying emotional luggage for the past two years. I attended Kunal's workshop and am already much better emotionally. I don't burst out at any given time. An awareness has built up, so I can get into a calm state with any unhappy or anxious emotions within no time. I did not know how unhealthy emotions were impacting my body. I am now aware of it. This workshop has given me a lot of clarity and tools to be at peace with myself."
- Grateful Client

"I will 300% recommend this Workshop to everyone as this has got me in:

1) Awareness of Self

2) Healed Heart

3) Corrected my way of thinking

4) Replacing unhealthy with healthy thoughts

5) How to handle my emotions and love and accept myself.

6) From my thinking of I CAN'T, I have discovered the Power of "I CAN ".

7) Above all this, what I was missing the most, I have started Believing; "I AM LOVABLE, I AM WORTHY & I AM POWERFUL "!!

God bless.!! I Pray for your success in Touching & Healing More Loves & Hugs" - Grateful Client

Chapter 21

Identify & Shift
Unhealthy Core Beliefs

"You are a product of what you've told yourself in the past. What you tell yourself now will determine who you become in the future."— *Jit Puru,*

Identify Unhealthy Core Beliefs

Core beliefs are your ideas and philosophies, which you profoundly and intensely hold on to. You may have developed these core beliefs in early childhood or based on specific events which could have happened in your life. These core beliefs can be negative or positive based on your learnings and life experiences. We want to look at identifying the unhealthy core beliefs and correcting them.

Step 1) Write your NAT or unhealthy thought.
Step 2) Ask yourself the below questions to dig deeper

What does this NAT mean about me?
Why is this a problem?
What is so bad about it?
What is the worst about it?
Keep asking the above questions till you narrow down your core belief.

Example 1

NAT - She is ignoring me
What does "She is ignoring me" mean about me?
That I am not attractive
What does "I am not attractive" mean about me?
That I am not getting attention
What is the worst about not getting attention?
That I will be lonely
What does being lonely mean about me?
That I am unlovable.

Example 2

NAT – My boss should have promoted me
What does "No promotion mean about me?
That my work was not worthy of getting a promotion
What does "my work not being worthy" mean about me?
That I am not a valuable employee
What does "not being a valuable employee" mean about me?
I am worthless

Recall the last unpleasant event which you experience which gave rise to unpleasant emotion. For that event, write down your NAT

_____

What does the above NAT mean about you?

_____

Why is this a problem?

_____

What is so bad about it?

_____

What is the worst about it?

_____

What is your core belief?

_____

If you found the above method challenging to implement, then do not worry. I have reduced the complexity. I have listed below the common unhealthy core beliefs and recommend placing your hands on your heart and slowly reading all of them. Notice any change in your emotion or body sensation when reading it aloud. Make a note of those core beliefs you think applies to you. Do not rush when you do this assessment. Take your time. You could take 3-4 days or even more just to do this assessment and that is okay.

List of Unhealthy Core Beliefs

- I am unlovable
- I am a failure
- I am good for nothing
- I am not good enough
- I am powerless.
- I am not worthy
- I need everyone to approve of me
- I must avoid being disliked by anyone
- I must succeed in everything to be valuable
- It's not ok to make mistakes. If I do, I'm a bad person
- Other people should strive to ensure I am always happy
- People who do not make me happy should be punished
- Things must work out the way I want them to
- Everyone needs to rely on someone stronger than them
- Events in my past are to blame for my attitudes and behavior's today
- My future outcomes will be the same as my past outcomes
- I shouldn't have to feel sad, discomfort, or pain
- Someone somewhere should take responsibility for me
- I am incompetent
- I did something bad, therefore I am a bad person
- I am unsafe
- I must be loved to be happy
- If other people dislike me, I can't be happy
- If I'm alone, I'll be lonely.
- I must do more than other people to be as good as them
- I can't trust other people because they'll hurt me

- If people know what I'm really like, they won't like me
- My happiness depends more on other people than on me
- If a person I want to love me doesn't, that means I'm unlovable
- I should always be modest about my abilities
- To be nice, I must help everyone in need
- I can't cope on my own
- I have no right to ask other people to help me
- It's my fault that those I love are in trouble
- I should think of other people first, even if I have difficulties
- I should never hurt anyone's feelings
- I'm basically bad (stupid, ugly, lazy, needy, demanding)
- I must have total control

Let's pause for a minute and reassess. You have noted the core beliefs that apply to you. You may now think that these core beliefs are true and that is how they are supposed to be. There is nothing wrong with it. Well, my friend, lets acknowledge that these are unhealthy core beliefs. You believe in them based on your past experiences and learnings and events. Now the choice is for you to unlearn and drop them. What you are experiencing could be a feeling of doubt or confusion. Core beliefs are so strong in nature that they may not allow us to differentiate between actual facts and what we believe as facts.

If you feel comfortable proceeding further to drop this belief and create a new healthy core belief, then continue to read further.

To bring in the shift, we will work only on one core belief at one time. Once we have achieved success in shifting it, then work on the next one.

Below are the steps to shift the old core belief with the new healthy core belief.

Shifting Unhealthy Core Belief

Step 1) State your old core belief.

The first step is to pen down the old core belief. For example, *I am a failure.*

Step 2) Create a New Healthy Realistic Belief

Create a new healthy and realistic core belief (this would be the opposite of the old core belief). The new core belief must be believable. For example, if your old core belief was *"I am a failure"* for 36 years, and now if you decide to set your new core belief as *"I am super successful"*, it may contradict your belief system. Your subconscious mind may reject this new belief. A more realistic belief could be *"I am not a total failure"*, *"I have been successful in a few areas"*, *"I have succeeded in some projects"*, or *"I achieved some success"*.

I have listed possible suggestions for new core beliefs from the previous list. Create your own or choose from the list I have mentioned after this chapter based on what works for you.

Step 3) Tap on the New Core Belief

Tap on all the body points with the new core belief as below:

KC: I am successful in doing a few projects
EB: I am successful in doing a few projects
SE: I am successful in doing a few projects
UE: I am successful in doing a few projects
UN: I am successful in doing a few projects
CH: I am successful in doing a few projects
CB: I am successful in doing a few projects
UA: I am successful in doing a few projects
AFT: I am successful in doing a few projects
ToH: I am successful in doing a few projects

Step 4) Create a Future Timeline Assessment

Assess how many days in a row would you have to feel this new positive belief for you to truly, deeply, and completely know that your new belief 100% holds true for you? Give it a count say it will take me 4 days or 300 days in a row to continuously feel/know that it is now a part of my belief system. For example, it will take me 28 days to truly and completely believe that "I am successful in doing few projects"

Step 5) Activate the Emotion from the New Core Belief in the Here and Now

Sit in a comfortable position with your eyes closed. Put yourself out that many days into the future so that you now feel and know that you truly, deeply and have entirely absorbed this new belief. Describe how you feel now. For example, when I put myself out on the 28th day truly believing that *"I am successful in doing few projects"* I feel very content.

Step 6) Identify your Learning
From this advantage point of now holding this new belief and new feeling, look back at the former version of yourself and describe yourself.

For example, When I look back, I feel sorry for myself that I had this belief that *"I am a failure"* for such a long time.

Step 7) Get Started to a Brighter Future
Come back to the present moment- knowing that you now believe in this new positive belief system you have created, how does the future feel to you from this moment forward?

For example, the future feels very positive, knowing that I am going to be successful

ILLUSTRATION
Step 1) State your old core belief
I am not good enough

Step 2) Create a New Healthy Realistic Belief
I am good enough

Step 3) Tap on the New Core Belief
Tap on all the body points with
"I am good enough"

Step 4) Create a Future Timeline Assessment
It will take me 48 days to continuously know / feel/
experience that I am good enough to entirely believe that
I am good enough

Step 5) Activate the Emotion from the New Core Belief in the Here and Now

I feel super awesome to believe that I am good enough.

Step 6) Identify your Learning

When I look back, I feel sad. I did not deserve to live my life with this belief.

Step 7) Get Started to a Brighter Future

I am confident to live a great life believing that I am good enough.

List of Unhealthy (Old) Vs Healthy (New)

Core Beliefs

Old: I am unlovable / I don't deserve love

New: I am lovable / I am getting to believe to be lovable / I deserve love

Old: I am good for nothing / I am not good enough

New: I am good with one thing / I am good with a few things/ I am deserving / I am good enough

Old: I am powerless

New: I have choices / I am powerful

Old: I am not worthy

New: I am worthy / I am worthwhile

Old: I need everyone to approve of me

New: I prefer people to approve of me however am okay if some don't / I am okay if people do not approve of me

Old: I must avoid being disliked by anyone

New: I am okay being disliked / I am okay being liked and disliked

Old: I must succeed in everything I do to be valuable

New: I prefer to succeed in everything I do however I could fail sometime. Failing does not make me any less valuable.

Old: It's not ok to make mistakes. If I do, I'm a bad person.

New: I am okay to make mistakes. It does not make me bad / I am a human being, and I can make mistakes. Mistakes does not define me.

Old: Other people should strive to ensure I am always happy

New: I am responsible for my happiness

Old: People should be punished who do not make me happy.

New: I do not hold other people accountable for my happiness

Old: Things must work out the way I want them to.

New: I wish things work out the way I want them, however I am okay if they don't

Old: Everyone needs to rely on someone stronger than them

New: Everyone is capable and self-sufficient / Asking for support does not make people dependent

Old: Events in my past are to blame for my attitudes and behavior's today

New: Events in my past have made be stronger and wise to deal with different life situations

Old: My future outcomes will be the same as my past outcomes

New: My future outcome is based on my decisions and actions I take in the present

Old: I shouldn't have to feel sad, discomfort or pain

New: It's okay to feel sad and discomfort

Old: Someone somewhere should take responsibility for me

New: I take joyful responsibility of me / I take my responsibility with Xyz area of my life

Old: I am incompetent

New: I am competent / I am competent in some things

Old: I did something bad, therefore I am a bad person.

New: Bad behaviors do not define me as a bad person / I am learning about my behaviors

Old: I am unsafe

New: I am believing to be safe in situations / I am safe

Old: I must be loved to be happy

New: I am capable to love myself and keep myself happy/ My happiness does not depend on others.

Old: If other people dislike me, I can't be happy.

New: I can start being happy even if others don't like me / I can be happy irrespective of other people liking or disliking me.

Old: If I'm alone, I'll be lonely.

New: Being along does not make me lonely

Old: I must do more than other people to be as good as them.

New: I choose to do my best with my own strengths. I take inspiration from others to improve myself.

Old: I can't trust other people because they'll hurt me.

New: I can gradually start trusting people.

Old: If people know what I'm really like, they won't like me.

New: I am okay if people know what I'm really like. I am okay if they choose to like me or not.

Old: My happiness depends more on other people than on me.

New: I am responsible for my happiness

Old: If a person I want to love me doesn't, that means I'm unlovable.

New: I am lovable / I deserve to love and be loved

Old: I should always be modest about my abilities
New: I choose to be wise talking about my abilities with people who truly would understand them

Old: To be nice, I must help everyone in need.
New: I am willing to help someone in need if it suits me / Helping or not does not define how nice I am

Old: I have no right to ask other people to help me.
New: I am okay to start asking for help from other people / Its okay to ask for help from others

Old: It's my fault that those I love are in trouble.
New: I am not fully responsible for others being in trouble

Old: I should think of other people first, even if I have difficulties.
New: I can think of other people first once I have looked after myself enough.

Old: I should never hurt anyone's feelings.
New: I prefer not to hurt anyone. However, I am willing to learn from it if I do.

Old: I'm bad (stupid, ugly, lazy, needy, demanding)
New: I am good enough / I am okay / I am independent

Old: I must have total control
New: Having total control is not needed

Old: I can't cope on my own.

New: I can cope with certain situations / I can cope on my own.

Chapter 22

Accepting Yourself and Your Reality

"Peace is something that comes from within. It is created by your willingness to accept yourself." — Jason Nelson

Nobody is perfect. No one's life is perfect. Suppose it is, then great. I haven't come across a single person who says that I am perfect, and my life is perfect. There are ups and downs. Sometimes you become thin, sometimes fat. Sometimes you succeed; sometimes you fail. Sometimes you get lucky, and sometimes luck does not favor you. Life is a series of such events (the good, the bad and the ugly). It is important that when such events are happening to you, then you do not resist them. Accept it and make peace with it.

- Gained 30 pounds? Accept yourself. Work towards losing weight.
- Lost your wallet. Accept it. Be aware next time
- Living in a small house. Accept it. Plan towards a bigger house and work towards it
- Spouse continuously nagging at you. Accept it and make peace with it. Work towards expanding your heart and understanding towards your spouse.
- Boss is not supporting you. Accept it. Work towards winning his confidence
- Made a big financial blunder. Accept it. Learn from your mistake. Become wise.

Below is tapping guidance which can help you accept yourself or your life reality.

Rounds 1 & 2) Tap on what you are not okay about yourself or about something you are resisting.

Round 3) Create a set-up statement and mention what you want to accept. Follow it up by saying I make peace with it.

- Even though I have gained 30 pounds, I accept myself and make peace with it
- Even though I lost my wallet, I accept and make peace with it.
- Even though I am living in a small house, I accept my house and make peace with it
- Even though my spouse is nagging, I accept my spouse and make peace with him/her.
- Even though my boss is not supporting me, I accept my boss and make peace with this situation.
- Even though I made a significant financial blunder, I accept it was a mistake and make peace with it.

If you do not know from where to start, you can accept yourself unconditionally. Here is a tapping script.

KC: I accept myself unconditionally, I accept myself unconditionally, I accept myself unconditionally
EB: I accept myself unconditionally, I accept myself unconditionally, I accept myself unconditionally
SE: I accept myself unconditionally, I accept myself unconditionally, I accept myself unconditionally

UE: I accept myself unconditionally, I accept myself unconditionally, I accept myself unconditionally
UN: I accept myself unconditionally, I accept myself unconditionally, I accept myself unconditionally
CH: I accept myself unconditionally, I accept myself unconditionally, I accept myself unconditionally
CB: I accept myself unconditionally, I accept myself unconditionally, I accept myself unconditionally
UA: I accept myself unconditionally, I accept myself unconditionally, I accept myself unconditionally

AFT: I accept myself unconditionally, I accept myself unconditionally, I accept myself unconditionally
ToH: I accept myself unconditionally, I accept myself unconditionally, I accept myself unconditionally

Want a voice for some push? Click here

Audio File: Accepting Yourself Unconditionally

(Listen on speaker for effective results)

Chapter 23

Create The Change

"The only thing constant is change" — Heraclitus

You can learn a million ways to be calm. However, if the external events or situations continue to bother you over a while and you see no scope for improvement, then it is time to make the change. In the earlier chapter, I explained the importance of acceptance. However, simply accepting and doing nothing about it does not help.

- Getting stressed at work? Change your job.
- Making significant and consistent losses in business, change your business or get back to employment for some time.
- Annoyed with the traffic situation, change the route.
- Fed up living in the same old house, move to a different home or a city.

Create that change that will create a positive impact in your life if you foresee no scope for improvements.

PART 3

PROACTIVE METHODS TO BE AT PEACE

Chapter 24

OM CHANTING TO CALM
THE MIND & BODY

"Omniscient, omnipotent, omnivorous and omnipresent all begin with OM"— Ashwin Sanghi

Chanting is an effective way of creating more peace in the mind and body. Chanting is a technique where you repeat one word or sentence, several times. Chanting "OM" can deliver excellent benefits in creating harmony in your mind and body.

The sound OM vibrates at a frequency similar to the vibrational frequency found throughout everything in nature. Hence when we chant OM, we are symbolically and physically tuning in to that sound and acknowledging our connection to all other living beings, nature, and the universe.

Beginning your day with OM chanting for 5-15 minutes can give you immense calmness throughout the day. When you sit for chanting, you need to chant AUM instead of OM. Here is a video that explains how to chant AUM which symbolizes OM.

AUM/ OM Chanting Video

Chapter 25

De-Cluttering Your Space

"When your room is clean and uncluttered, you have no choice but to examine your inner state." – Marie Kondo.

The environment you live or work matters.
De-clutter your space. I am not an expert in de-cluttering; hence, I request you to use your method to de-clutter your space. It is essential to see your surrounding as neat. Your environment can bring clarity, joy, and calmness once it is de-cluttered, organized, and tidy.

I am going to suggest a way for you to get started. Just take a walk in the house/space you intend to de-clutter. Take a walk in the living room, kitchen, bedroom, garage, and storeroom. While you walk, scan the entire area, and fill several boxes with the items you are confident of getting rid of it quickly and easily. You are looking for quick and easy decisions at this point. Grab the things you know you can undoubtedly get rid of in plain view. Once you have filled the boxes, you can later decide which ones you want to discard and which ones you want to donate to charity. The next step is to look for oversized items that take up much space – cardboard boxes, extensive tools, bicycles, and furniture. Remove the ones which you do not need. Doing the above steps gets you started. You can then proceed with whatever method you want to de-clutter your home or space.

Chapter 26

Knowledge & Experts

While this book has several solutions to make you calm for events and emotions you experience every day, you still need to take action to resolve issues for which you may not be an expert. Experts in professions – Doctor, lawyer, real estate consultant, Chartered Accountant, plumber, electrician, mechanic, animal communicator. It would be best to have a good network of such experts. You never know when you may need to use their services. Below is the list of professionals. You may choose the ones you want to start building your connections with or at least know someone whom you can contact if needed.

Accountant, Actor /Actress, Architect, Astronomer, Author, Baker, Bricklayer, Bus driver, Butcher, Carpenter, Chef/Cook, Cleaner, Dentist, Doctor, Dustman/Refuse collector, Electrician, Engineer, Factory worker, Farmer, Fireman/Firefighter, Fisherman, Florist, Gardener, Hairdresser, Journalist, Judge, Lawyer, Lecturer, Librarian, Lifeguard, Mechanic, Model, Newsreader, Nurse, Optician, Painter, Pharmacist, Photographer, Pilot, Plumber, Politician, Policeman/Policewoman, Postman, Real estate agent, Receptionist, Scientist, Secretary, Shop assistant, Soldier, Tailor, Taxi driver, Teacher, Translator, Traffic warden, Travel agent, Veterinary doctor, Waiter/Waitress, Window cleaner etc.

Knowledge is Power

- Do you get frustrated when you get stuck in traffic for an hour? Find out if there is any quicker way to reach your work.
- Do you get stressed when you struggle to cook food? Find out if there is an easy way to make your meal.
- Do you get anxious while creating a sales presentation on PowerPoint? Then, find out if there is any faster way to make a good presentation.
- Do you fear visiting the dentist for a root canal? Find out the procedure of root canal and a good dentist.
- Do you get nervous before your exams? The plan and prepare much in advance.

I am sharing these examples to state a very simple point-Knowledge is Power. You can use all the techniques in this book; however, you must do the tasks for day-to-day living.

- You must travel to work (unless you can work from home).
- You must cook your food (unless you order from outside).
- You must make the presentation (unless you find another job)
- You must get your root canal done. (Unless you are okay with rotten teeth)
- You must study to pass your exams. (Unless you are okay to fail.)

You have got to do it! No excuses. To do these tasks better and be less stressed, gain knowledge. Become knowledgeable and powerful.

Chapter 27

Magical Tool to
Lift Your Spirit Everyday

"We Are Lovable. Even if the most important person in your world rejects you, you are still real, and you are still okay." — *Melody Beattie*

Many of our unhealthy core beliefs are based on being helpless, worthless & unlovable. Tapping on the below magical affirmation three times in a day – morning, afternoon, and evening can create wonders in your life.

Round 1

KC: I am lovable, worthy, and powerful. I am lovable, worthy, and powerful. I am lovable, worthy, and powerful.
EB: I am lovable, worthy, and powerful. I am lovable, worthy, and powerful. I am lovable, worthy, and powerful.
SE: I am lovable, worthy, and powerful. I am lovable, worthy, and powerful. I am lovable, worthy, and powerful.
UE: I am lovable, worthy, and powerful. I am lovable, worthy, and powerful. I am lovable, worthy, and powerful.
UN: I am lovable, worthy, and powerful. I am lovable, worthy, and powerful. I am lovable, worthy, and powerful.
CH: I am lovable, worthy, and powerful. I am lovable, worthy, and powerful. I am lovable, worthy, and powerful.
CB: I am lovable, worthy, and powerful. I am lovable, worthy, and powerful. I am lovable, worthy, and powerful.

UA: I am lovable, worthy, and powerful. I am lovable, worthy, and powerful. I am lovable, worthy, and powerful. **AFT:** I am lovable, worthy, and powerful. I am lovable, worthy, and powerful. I am lovable, worthy, and powerful. **ToH:** I am lovable, worthy, and powerful. I am lovable, worthy, and powerful. I am lovable, worthy, and powerful.

If tapping on these core beliefs makes you uncomfortable, you may need to do some introspection. Revisit the chapter on shifting core beliefs.

This magic tool is like a counterattack to your unhealthy core belief. For example, one participant complained that she did not believe she was powerful during my workshop. We worked together using the EFT + CBT model, and she could identify the reason for being powerless. Once we diluted her old core belief, she could do the tapping very comfortably.

Let us do this awesome tapping together. Click here

Audio File: I am Lovable, Worthy & Powerful

(Listen on speaker for effective results

Chapter 28

Being Grateful

"Do not spoil what you have by desiring what you have not; remember that what you now have was once among the things you only hoped for."— Epicurus

Our life revolves around *What I Have* and *What I Want*. The *I Want List* includes - A bigger house, car, dream job, more money, better health and relationships and your entire bucket list. The *I Have List* includes everything, and everybody present in your life.

This cycle of *"I want this"* and *"I have this"* keeps changing with time, priorities, and circumstances. As we are continuously evolving each day, it is important to express gratitude to our *I Have List* while we progress towards achieving the *I Want List*.

EFT tapping expressing gratitude for everything which you have does wonders. Here you deep dive into your heart and start tapping on everything and everybody present in your life who is contributing to your life. With gratitude towards your, *I Have List*; you will experience a great sense of calmness towards your *I Want List*. Your progress will become faster.

Start tapping and talking about your I Have List by saying it aloud. There are no rules for gratitude tapping. Do as many rounds as you would like. Have fun. Enjoy doing it.

KC: I am grateful for the clothes that comforts me

EB: I am thankful for the house for shelter

SE: I am grateful for the car that makes my travel easy

UE: I am thankful for my loving wife for her significant contribution

UN: I am thankful for the support of my dad

CH: I am grateful that my mom cares about me

CB: I am grateful for the remarkable friend who is always there

UA: I am thankful to have a great mentor in my life

AFT: I am grateful for the skills I possess

ToH: I am grateful that I have a job

KC: I am grateful for the food I eat

EB: I thank the cook who makes my meal

SE: I am grateful to my gym trainer

UE: I am thankful to my friend for always being around

UN: I am grateful that my job pays my bills

CH: I am grateful that my boss helps me greatly

CB: I am thankful that my business is growing

UA: I am grateful to receive help from the stranger who gave me a ride

AFT: I am grateful for such a beautiful weather.

ToH: I am grateful for the books I read

Chapter 29

Forgiveness

"Forgiveness is not an occasional act; it is a constant attitude."— *Martin Luther King Jr.*

Have you ever spoken with your worry? You read it right. Not ABOUT your worry but with your worry? A technique where you talk to your concern or what is bothering you the most and ask for forgiveness. It can miraculously open things in your universe by healing or clearing various known or unknown blockages.

You ask for forgiveness by tapping on all the body points and saying, "I am sorry, please forgive me, thank you, I love you, I forgive myself", to the issue bothering you. For example, if you are trying to sell your house for a long time without success, say, "Dear House, I am sorry, please forgive me, thank you, I love you, I forgive myself". With this prayer, your house could get sold immediately. I do not know. Be open to miracles. You could bump into a real estate consultant who has a client waiting to buy your house. You could get some clarity to increase or decrease the selling price. You could get an idea to start a business from your home. Several possibilities open when you clear the energy blocks with this technique. You may need to say this forgiveness prayer just once or for many days or months. Use your intuition. Similarly, you can do forgiveness for different goals and intentions in your life. Examples are as below:

- *Dear Book, followed by the prayer. (To quickly publish your book)*
- *Dear Weight, (To lose or gain weight as per your intention)*
- *Dear House (to buy, sell or rent a house)*
- *Dear Wife (To improve your relationship with your wife)*
- *Dear Situation (To improve your overall life situation or related a specific are- health, relationships, finance etc.)*
- *Dear Work (To do well at work or find new opportunities to expand)*
- *Dear Boss (To enhance your relationship)*
- *Dear Business (To bring in more harmony in your business or to expand it)*
- *Dear Job (To create more peace in your existing job or find a new job)*
- *Dear Family (To create more love, peace, and harmony within the family)*
- *Dear Child (To conceive or improve your relationship with your child)*
- *Dear Studies (To focus and study)*
- *Dear Marriage (To get married or make your marriage work or to end your marriage peacefully based on your intent)*
- *Dear Father (To heal your relationship with your father) So can you do with any other person / relationship.*

When you say the forgiveness prayer, it is crucial to keep the intention in mind. For example, when you say, "Dear Money, I am sorry, please forgive me, thank you, I love you,

I forgive myself". What is your intention? Is it to clear your debts, increase revenue, increase revenue sources like creating passive income, build upon your savings, reduce expenses or all of it? Be clear with the intent, and then tap on the prayer.

You can use this technique for almost everything that is bothering you. For example, not getting a cab to reach the office, say Dear Cab and the forgiveness prayer, not getting the right clothes when you are shopping, say Dear shopping or Dear clothes followed by the prayer. Unable to find the house keys say Dear House keys and so on. Below is an example of tapping with the intent to lose weight.

KC: Dear Weight, I am sorry, please forgive me, thank you, I love you, I forgive myself.
EB: Dear Weight, I am sorry, please forgive me, thank you, I love you, I forgive myself.
SE: Dear Weight, I am sorry, please forgive me, thank you, I love you, I forgive myself.
UE: Dear Weight, I am sorry, please forgive me, thank you, I love you, I forgive myself.
UN: Dear Weight, I am sorry, please forgive me, thank you, I love you, I forgive myself.
CH: Dear Weight, I am sorry, please forgive me, thank you, I love you, I forgive myself.
CB: Dear Weight, I am sorry, please forgive me, thank you, I love you, I forgive myself.
UA: Dear Weight, I am sorry, please forgive me, thank you, I love you, I forgive myself.

AFT: Dear Weight, I am sorry, please forgive me, thank you, I love you, I forgive myself.

ToH: Dear Weight, I am sorry, please forgive me, thank you, I love you, I forgive myself.

Here is a tapping voice to help you do forgiveness with your father. Play it on speaker for effective results.

Acknowledgements

Dear Reader, I Thank You for reading this book (and listening to the audios) and allowing me to contribute to your life through this book.

I am most grateful to Mr. Gary Craig, who invented the Emotional Freedom Technique, Dr Aaron T. Beck for Cognitive Behavior Therapy, and my numerous clients who validated the techniques mentioned in this book. Your feedback has given me confidence and encouragement to write this book.

I am grateful to my parents for their blessings and guiding light from heaven above. I express my deep gratitude to my wife Rashmi for being a great support and to my cute little daughter Maahi; both have played a pivotal role by just being there with me in all my life's ups and downs.

I am grateful to my teachers, Mr Prasenjit & Debosmita. I could not have asked for a better teacher. Your guidance and techniques have immensely helped me get a good grip on both the therapies and made my journey to write this book a lot easier. I also would like to call out the names of those individuals who have contributed immensely to various aspects of my life, both personally & professionally.

- Suzy Woo for always supporting me on the professional and personal front.
- Graham Nicholls for sharing in-depth knowledge on EFT

- Kain Ramsay for the incredible course on CBT
- Center of Excellence & Endorphin for their brilliant training
- Matthew Barnett for learning NLP
- Nitin Soni and Som Batla for teaching me the tricks and trade of writing a book
- Vigneshwari Abraham has inspired me constantly.
- Jerry Sargeant for his teachings in Star Magic.
- My batch mates of leadership training programs
- Krishan Kakrecha for designing the book cover

I take the opportunity to thank my incredible family, friends and well-wishers for their continued support – My Family (Gulab, Kirti, Sunita, Karishma, Akshay, Megha, Shantanu, Amita, Vishal, Ranjit, Priya) and my friends - Swati, Khushi, Bushra, Bhakti, Rahul, Kavita, Rushabh, Shweta, Makarand, Niraj, Varsha, Prakruti and all the others who helped me in the past and those who will stand by me in the future.

I have been inspired by reading the below books and received some amazing insights for writing this book. I would highly recommend reading them:

- Cognitive Behavioural Therapy Workbook for Dummies – Rhena Branch & Rob Willson
- Feeling Good – David D Burns
- Tapping The Healer Within- Roger Callahan
- EFT for Weight Loss – Gary Craig
- The Tapping Solution: A Revolutionary System for Stress-Free Living – Nick Ortner & Mark Hyman

- The EFT manual -Dawson Church
- The Tapping Solution: For Weight Loss & Body Confidence – Jessica Ortner
- The Book of Tapping – Sophie Merle

About The Author

Kunal Dudeja (KD) is from Mumbai, India. By heart he is a trainer who believes in empowering and training people with EFT and CBT tools and techniques. His mission is to train people on the EFT+ CBT model, written in his book as he firmly believes that every human should learn this skill to get better at managing their thoughts and emotions for improved mental peace and emotional wellbeing.

KD has worked with thousands of clients across India, United States, and Dubai with one-on-one consultation as well as through empowering workshops.

He conducts his online sessions with simplicity and gives each participant their own space to learn and grow. His service offerings include conducting workshops on *Calm The Chaotic Mind* and *EFT sessions for Weight Loss*.

Visit us to know more about our service offerings at www.kunaldudeja.com or write us kunaldudejacoach@gmail.com

Made in the USA
Monee, IL
13 October 2022

15799673R00075